CONTEN

CW00434661

Investigating Instructions: Instructional texts tell you what to do, and how to do it. They often come with illustrations to make things clearer. Sometimes they make you scratch your head in confusion! This unit will teach you all about good and bad instructional texts, both written and spoken.

Smoky Sweetcorn Soup with Lime Butter

For the soup
4 sweetcorn cobs

4 tbs olive oil

1 onion, chopped

2 garlic cloves, chopped

250 g potato, chopped

900 ml vegetable stock

300 ml milk, warmed

pinch of cayenne pepper

salt and pepper

For the butter
125 g butter

grated rind and juice of 1 lime

2 tbs fresh coriander, chopped

1. First make the lime butter. In a small bowl beat together the butter, lime rind, lime juice and the coriander until evenly combined. Add a little salt and pepper to taste and roll into a log shape. Wrap in foil and refrigerate until required.

2. Strip away the outer leaves of the corn, brush each cob with oil and sprinkle with salt and pepper. Grill for 15 minutes, turning frequently until charred on all sides. Remove from the heat and leave to cool slightly.

3. Heat the remaining oil in a saucepan and fry the onion and garlic for 5 minutes until softened, then add the potato and fry for a further 5 minutes.

4. Hold the corn cobs vertically and cut downwards to remove the kernels; add to the saucepan with the stock and milk. Bring to the boil, cover, and simmer gently for 30 minutes. Transfer to a liquidizer and process until the soup is smooth.

5. Return the soup to the pan, add the cayenne and salt and pepper and heat through gently. Serve hot, garnished with thin slices of lime butter.

CHICKEN CORN CHOWDER
FOR ONE

INGREDIENTS

* 2 spring onions
* small knob of butter or margarine
* 50 g boneless cooked chicken
* 200 g cream-style sweetcorn
* 50 ml milk
* salt and pepper
* a few packet croutons

* Cut any bad bits off the spring onions, then wash and dry them. Cut them across into small pieces. Put a small knob of butter or margarine in a saucepan. Put the pan on the hob, and the heat to low.

* When the butter has melted, add the spring onion. Stir, then leave to cook very gently for 5 minutes. While the onion is cooking, remove any skin from the chicken. Cut the chicken into small pieces.

* Add the chicken to the spring onion. Stir in the cream-style sweetcorn. Pour in the milk and stir to mix. Add a little salt and pepper. Increase the heat to medium and heat the soup until it is just bubbling. Cook for 2 minutes, stirring.

* Turn the heat off and pour the soup into a bowl. Sprinkle packet croutons over the top.

HIGHWAY CODE

Rules for cyclists

45. Clothing. You should wear
- a cycle helmet which conforms to current regulations
- appropriate clothes for cycling. Avoid clothes which may get tangled in the chain, or in a wheel or may obscure your lights
- light-coloured or fluorescent clothing which helps other road users to see you in daylight and poor light
- reflective clothing and/or accessories (belt, arm or ankle bands) in the dark

46. At night your cycle **MUST** have front and rear lights lit. It **MUST** also be fitted with a red rear reflector (and amber pedal reflectors, if manufactured after 1/10/85). White front reflectors and spoke reflectors will also help you to be seen …

50. You MUST obey all traffic signs and traffic light signals.

51. You should
- keep both hands on the handlebars except when signalling or changing gear
- keep both feet on the pedals
- not ride more than two abreast
- ride in single file on narrow or busy roads
- not ride close behind another vehicle
- not carry anything that will affect your balance or may get tangled up with your wheels or chain

52. You should
- look all around before moving away from the kerb, turning or manoeuvring, to make sure it is safe to do so. Give a clear signal to show other road users what you intend to do
- look well ahead for obstructions in the road, such as drains, pot-holes and parked vehicles … and watch out for doors being opened in your path

No cycling   No right turn

No entry for vehicles   Stop and give way

Only
Buses and cycles only   Route to be used by pedal cycles only

ARRIVE ALIVE

Before you set off

☺ Make sure your cycle is safe to ride – your brakes and tyres should be working well.

☺ Always wear a **cycle helmet** – it will help to protect you if you have an accident.

☺ Make sure that other road users can see you. Wear fluorescent materials in daylight and at dusk, and something **reflective** at night.

☺ Riding a bike which is too big or too small can affect your balance ...

On your bike

☺ Before starting off, turning right or left, overtaking or stopping, you must look behind and make sure it is safe and then give a clear arm signal to show what you intend to do.

☺ You must not ride on the pavement unless there are special signs allowing you to do so.

☺ When you get on your cycle look all round for traffic. When it is safe to move off, cycle away.

☺ Always keep both hands on the handlebars unless you are signalling or changing gears.

☺ When turning from one road into another, pedestrians who are crossing that road have the right of way, so give way.

☺ You must obey traffic light signals and road signs, and the signals made by police officers, traffic wardens or school crossing patrols.

Velociraptor

DINOFILE

Velociraptor was one of the most savage killers. It would usually team up to attack and was equipped with razor-sharp fangs, claws like grappling hooks, powerful jaws for tearing flesh and muscular legs to stamp the life out of small prey.

Height	1m
Weight	15kg
Length	2m
Killer Rating	9
Intelligence Rating	10
Age (Million Years)	85

How to play Top Trumps

Any number of people can play. Shuffle and deal all the cards face down. Each player holds the cards so that they can see the top card only.

The player to the dealer's left starts by reading out an item from their top card (e.g. Weight 15kg). The other players then read out the same item. The one with the best or highest value wins and places all the top cards including their own to the bottom of their pile. It is then their turn again to choose an item from the next card.

If two or more cards share the top value or no data is available for that particular subject then all the cards are placed in the middle and the same player chooses again from the next card. The winner of the hand takes the cards in the middle as well.

The person with all the cards at the end is the winner.

HOW TO DRAW CARTOONS

FIRST FACES

All you need is a pencil and a sheet of paper. If you want to colour the faces in, you can use crayons or felt tips.

Draw a circle. Do two pencil lines crossing it. Put the nose where the lines cross. The ears are level with the nose.

The eyes go slightly above the nose. Rub out the lines crossing the face. Add any sort of hair you like.

FACES TO COPY

Here are some more faces for you to copy. You can see how in a cartoon some things are exaggerated, such as the size of the nose or the expression.

Mobile recycling envelope

recycle

your old mobile phone

RECYCLOX
FREEPOST LON1952
PO BOX 123456
London
SW71 9ZZ

All you need to do:
1. Place your old or redundant mobile handset in this envelope (please remove your SIM card).
2. Fill out the tear off strip at the top of the envelope & place it INSIDE the envelope with the phone.
3. Seal & simply put the envelope in the post. There is NO postage to pay.
4. RECYCLOX will recycle your mobile phone.

A maximum of 5 phones per customer

PLEASE ENSURE ALL SIM CARDS ARE REMOVED PRIOR TO POSTING THE PHONE – ANY SIM CARDS RECEIVED BY RECYCLOX WILL BE DESTROYED.

VISUAL INSTRUCTIONS

Assemble a Kinder Egg toy.

K03n°64

K03 n°65

Assemble an office chair.

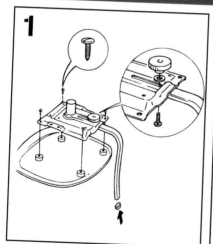

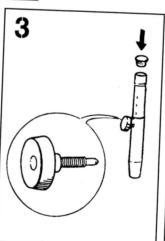

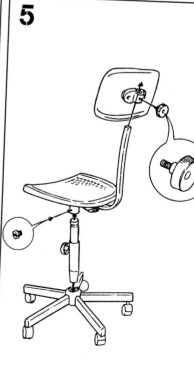

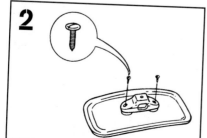

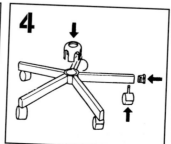

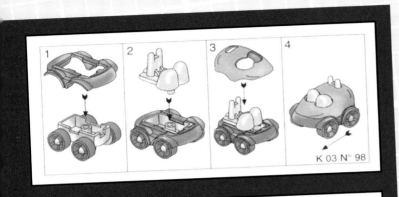

1 2 3 4

K 03 N° 98

K 03 N° 98

K 03 N° 99

K 03 N° 100

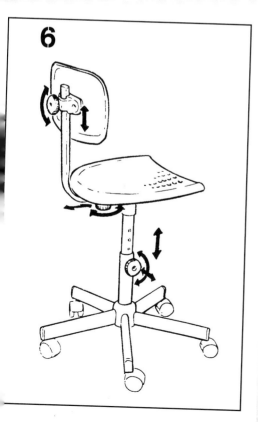

6

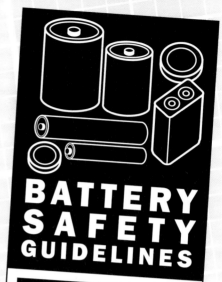

BATTERY SAFETY GUIDELINES

NEVER

Never attempt to recharge ordinary batteries, either in a charger or by applying heat to them. They may leak, cause fire or even explode. There are special rechargeable batteries which are clearly marked as such.

Battery safety rules

ALWAYS

Seek medical advice if you believe a cell has been swallowed. Cells are highly toxic.

Reviewing Recounts: A recount is a description of something that has happened. Some recounts are formal, some are informal. For example, someone writing a formal recount of an event will present it in a different way from someone telling a friend about it.

Thargon Starship 'Betamax'

Captain's Log, Inter-Galactic Date: Zyglot1m/xi@05 (Thurs)

We passed into Planet Football's gravitational field at 6.08 deltas, above a landmass known locally as 'Europe'. Travelling in a north-westerly direction at Warp Factor 62, we remained unobserved ourselves. But in the darkness below we clearly detected – at 324 separate locations – religious ceremonies being conducted in floodlit temples or 'stadiums'. Some contained many thousands of seated human worshippers.

At 6.09 deltas we entered the airspace of our target island, which is named 'Britain (Home of Football)'. This is the source of the brief TV transmissions of Match of the Day that we have picked up back on Planet Tharg.

Between 6.09 and 6.12 deltas we flew at reconnaissance height over Britain. We braked and became visible above the most impressive stadium – a cathedral we recognised from TV images as 'Old Trafford, Manchester'. Our scanners informed us that a holy 'game' was about to begin: the Red Devils v the Saints.

Our understanding of the religion of this primitive race is still far from complete. In order to further our research, it was our intention to land, introduce ourselves and observe an entire game. Our presence, however, caused unrest among the worshippers and their uniformed priests. One high official – possibly an archbishop – made a gesture towards us which we could only interpret as hostile. Wishing at this stage of our mission not to offend the human natives, we therefore decided to move on and seek a less sacred place to land.

From: Ariel Galapagob <arig@thargnet.comet>
To: Galapagobfamily@thargnet.comet
Subject: Mission to Planet Football
Date: Zyglot7m/xii@05 (Tues)

Dear All,

We're coming to the end of our week here on Planet Football and the natives could not have been more friendly. (Compared with missions to certain other solar systems, this one has been – as the humans say – 'a piece of gâteau', 'an absolute hoddle'!)

We've gathered masses of data about the planet, its life-forms, leisure activities and, of course, its religion. At a school we visited in Stratford-upon-Avon, some small humans tried to teach us the basic laws of football. Then we played a short practice 'game' against them, and we WON by 4 'goals' to 3!

Last night we were invited to a festival called Bonfire Night. All over Britain on this night, fake humans are burned on fires and there are huge bangs and flashes.

Tomorrow, our last day, we will play another 'game' – this time against the 'policemen' who have so kindly escorted us everywhere. The game will take place in the Millennium Stadium, Cardiff, before a crowd of 70,000 worshippers! Keep your toes crossed that we give a good performance.

Missing you all. (Don't forget to feed my silverfish!)

Love, Ariel

Downtown Sporting Pink

10th OCTOBER 2004

STARBURSTS SNAP JETS' WINNING STREAK!

Ed Fletcher applauds the rise in the fortunes of local Basketball team.

The latest signing of 6ft 9in forward, Frankie 'Sky-hi' Fixter to Downtown Starbursts has taken their game to new heights with a 98–91 victory against league front runners the Inter City Jets. The game tipped off at 7.30pm Tuesday, in front of a capacity crowd at Wellrun Stadium as the 'Bursts blasted out of the blocks with the first nine points of the game.

The second quarter saw some outstanding passes from the Jets' centre, Harry 'Sweet Pea' Holden, resulting in three well deserved points from a basket shot taken from behind and putting the Jets ahead of the game.

During half-time the crowd were treated to a spectacular slam dunk exhibition by the visiting New York Hot Shots.

Early in the second half the 'Bursts eased ahead as the Jets' confidence was downed after their forward, Snap Swingman, was fouled out by the referee. Scenting victory, the Starbursts went on to bag a bundle of baskets, finishing the game with a 7-point lead.

A spectacular slam dunk exhibition.

The Diary of a Victorian Apprentice

18th March, 1846 (Early Morning)

Yesterday was hectic. I got off Jem's cart outside the Reverend Screde's rectory. I hope never to endure again such a night of misery. He and his wife said long prayers for me and everyone else who worked for that heathen abomination, the railway works. The house was cold, the dinner awful, the bed lumpy. I hope I find good lodgings soon so I need never go near the Scredes again!

I must leave early to be at the works' entrance in time. From the rectory I can see the station and the great factory. The line to Bristol stretches away to the left and there is a train steaming along it. Beyond the station, the line to Gloucester and Cheltenham curves away. Swindon works lies in the angle made by the junction between the two. The great, long workshops, the smoke from boilers and steam hammers – even from here the busy noise and bustle make me shiver with excitement!

From *The Diary of A Victorian Apprentice* by Dennis Hamley

 **Project Team Meeting: 28 July 2004**

Minutes

Present: Angela M, Debra O, Fiona G, Ian J, Jeanne M, Raegan M
Apologies: Paul S

Action

1. Matters arising
- Since the last meeting (2 June 2004), progress has been made on the book covers. Design now OK, and images for individual books have been found.

  Debbie to show covers at usual weekly meeting.

2. Schedules
- Books 1, 3 and 4 are all running to schedule and the team should meet the handover date.
- Book 2 is running two weeks late as further research is required.

  Raegan to meet with author 4 August.

3. Printing
- Printers have been booked. Advance copies are due on 5 January.

  Jeanne to obtain quotes.

4. Date of next meeting
- 30 September, 3pm. Boardroom.

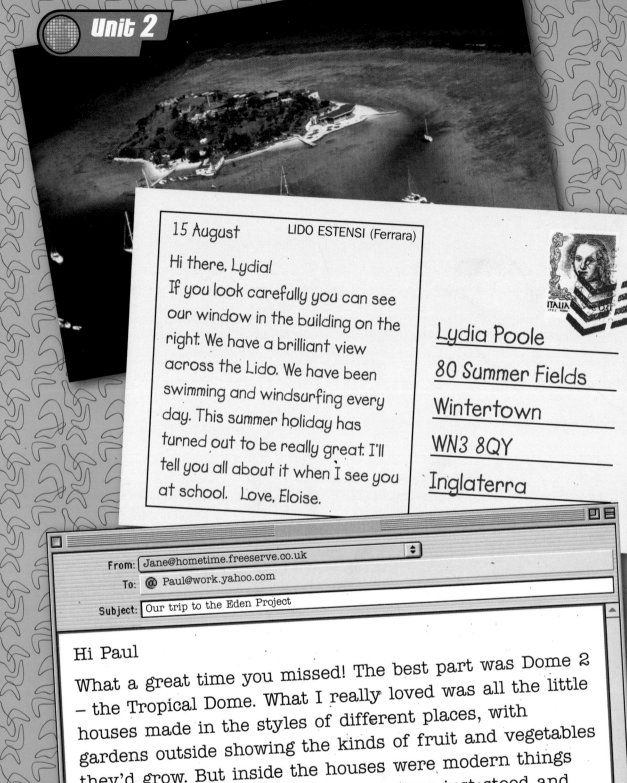

15 August   LIDO ESTENSI (Ferrara)

Hi there, Lydia!
If you look carefully you can see
our window in the building on the
right. We have a brilliant view
across the Lido. We have been
swimming and windsurfing every
day. This summer holiday has
turned out to be really great. I'll
tell you all about it when I see you
at school.   Love, Eloise.

Lydia Poole
80 Summer Fields
Wintertown
WN3 8QY
Inglaterra

ITALIA

From: Jane@hometime.freeserve.co.uk
To: @ Paul@work.yahoo.com
Subject: Our trip to the Eden Project

Hi Paul

What a great time you missed! The best part was Dome 2 – the Tropical Dome. What I really loved was all the little houses made in the styles of different places, with gardens outside showing the kinds of fruit and vegetables they'd grow. But inside the houses were modern things like TVs. It was boiling hot, so everyone just stood and panted when they got to the waterfall at the end of the path. Next time YOU MUST COME!! NO EXCUSES!!

Love Jane

PS a bunch of roses for you
~'~~,~{@ ~'~~,~{@ ~'~~,~{@ ~'~~,~{@ ~'~~,~{@

DOES THE EARTH SPIN?

Our challenge
- To show that the Earth spins on its axis.
- To demonstrate night and day in different parts of the world.

What we used
- a spinning globe
- a torch or strong light source
- thick card
- sticky tape
- scissors

What we did
We used a torch as the Sun. We stuck a cardboard figure on the globe in Australia and a cardboard figure on the globe in the UK. We shone the torch on Australia, then we spun the globe so that the torch shone on the UK.

What we found
When we shone the torch on Australia it was dark in the UK. We had to spin the globe to make it light in the UK. When we did this it was dark in Australia.

The outcome

Every part of the world has day and night. This means that the Earth has to spin so that each part of it faces the Sun.

So when it's day on one side of the world it's night on the other.

It spins round once every 24 hours.

ALIEN INVASION!

Exploring Explanations: Explanatory texts often deal with how or why something happens, and give reasons. They therefore contain factual information. Written explanations are usually quite formal – spoken ones can be more informal, especially if you are talking to friends or family.

LOCALMERE DOG CLUB
Annual Show, 24–25 May

Due to unavoidable circumstances, this year's Show has had to be cancelled.

Unfortunately, Mrs Goodboy, the trainer, has suffered a broken leg following an and a lost whistle following an incident with a stray dog. The rosettes have had to be destroyed at short notice following a break-in by some local pups; and in a suspected linked incident, the doggy treats have also gone missing.

We do apologize for any disappointment or inconvenience caused. All tickets will, of course, be refunded. Please see Mrs Fanshawe at the village shop.

We hope that, next year, the Show will take place as normal.

Stafford B Terrier

Sir Stafford Bulle Terrier, Chairman

10 GOOD REASONS TO EXERCISE!

1. It tones your body
2. It strengthens your heart and joints
3. It reduces stress
4. It makes you more supple
5. It makes you more resistant to disease
6. It keeps you fit and active
7. It improves your posture
8. It improves your confidence
9. It's fun!
10. It's an investment in your future

What are you waiting for?

DESIGNED FOR FEET

The modern trainer is a very high tech creation. It has five separate elements, which all work together to keep your foot comfortable and help prevent injuries.

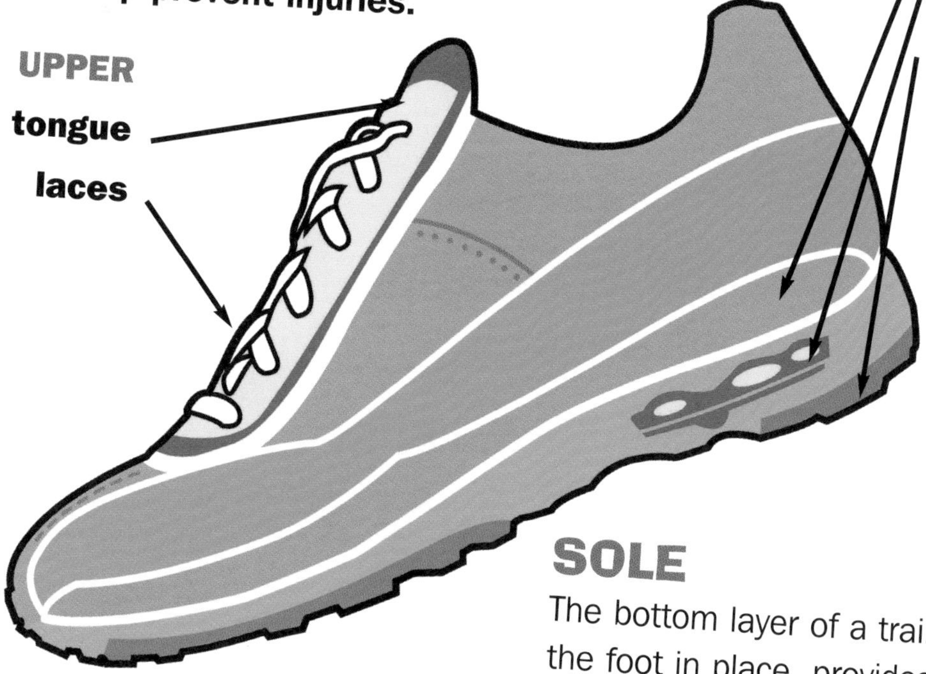

UPPER

tongue

laces

SOLE

insole

midsole

outsole

SOLE

The bottom layer of a trainer holds the foot in place, provides padding, and keeps the foot from slipping.

UPPER

The upper part holds the sole against the bottom of your foot. It will be made of canvas, leather or nylon. It works with the midsole, to keep your foot steady so it doesn't twist too much.

Laces: These keep the shoe on your foot. Velcro straps instead of laces are popular, too.

Tongue: The tongue stops the laces from digging into your instep.

Insole: This thin foam insert also provides some padding, but its main job is to keep your foot in place inside the trainer.

Midsole: This thick, springy foam rubber section serves as a cushion for your foot. Some have special features like air pockets to increase the cushioning.

Outsole: This layer of tough rubber grips the ground, giving you traction as you walk.

STATIC ELECTRICITY

When electric charges build up on something like a balloon, they've got nowhere to go so they just sit there. This is called static electricity (static means 'not moving'). The charges don't really like doing this. They're always looking for a way to move. Dip a charged balloon in water and all the charges will jump off the balloon and into the water!

WHAT A SHOCK

Have you ever had a little shock when getting out of a car? When a car rushes through the air, it can get charged up. The electric charges can't travel through the rubber tyres on the wheels, so the charge has nowhere to go. When you get out of the car and touch the ground, the electric charges jump off the car and into you!

HOW A TOASTER WORKS

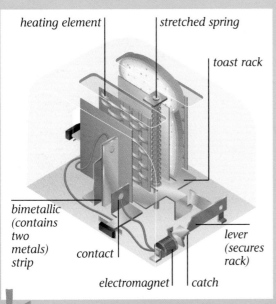

heating element | stretched spring

toast rack

bimetallic (contains two metals) strip

contact

electromagnet | catch

lever (secures rack)

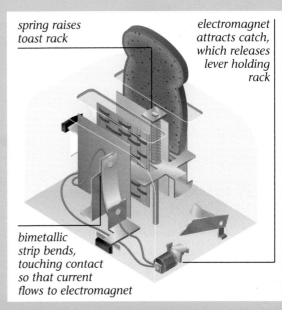

spring raises toast rack

electromagnet attracts catch, which releases lever holding rack

bimetallic strip bends, touching contact so that current flows to electromagnet

ANIMAL BEHAVIOUR

Corner House
1 Fore Street
Levelend
BC12 1QT

Tuesday 8 June

Dear Mr Glum,

I am sorry that you weren't happy with James' homework this morning. James did attempt to complete his work on animal behaviour, but we suffered a rather unfortunate series of events.

James was bending over his school bag, innocently getting out his books, when next door's overgrown monster of a cat ran in through the hallway and jumped on James' back.

James, as you know, has an understandable horror of cats (if you recall, the cat has tormented the poor boy on numerous other occasions), and so reacted rather badly. The schoolbag went flying through the window along with James, just as the dog from the other side came crashing through the garden.

Seizing the opportunity to bite something (as he'd missed the cat), the brutish dog ran off with the bag. Thankfully, he didn't get James as well.

By the time we'd caught up with the dog, James was so out of puff (and suffering from several cuts and bruises, not to mention concussion) that he really wasn't in a fit state to do anything more than have a sit down. Just as well, really, as the dog dived into the local pond after a stick. Which is why James' work was rather soggy.

Yours sincerely,

Rosemary de la Foole

Rosemary de la Foole
(James' mum)

30 July 2004

IMPORTANT PRODUCT RECALL NOTICE

Mega Pasta Sauce from Tortelli Foods 185g small glass jar

Quality Testing checks have revealed that some **185g small jars of Mega Pasta Sauce** from **Tortelli Foods** do not meet our normal high standards of product quality.

A minor ingredient (cayenne pepper) has been shown to cause mild stomach problems. As a precautionary measure only, we are temporarily recalling this product.

WHAT YOU SHOULD DO

If you have purchased a 185g jar of Mega Pasta Sauce, please contact the Freephone number below, where one of our personal advisors will provide information on how to obtain your product replacement voucher. Please do not return the jar to your retailer.

We apologise for any inconvenience caused and would like to thank all our customers in advance for their co-operation. We are working to restore this product to its normal high quality as soon as possible.

FREEPHONE RECALL NUMBER 0800 12345

APPLIES ONLY TO MEGA PASTA SAUCE FROM TORTELLI FOODS

PLEASE NOTE THAT NO OTHER TORTELLI FOODS ARE AFFECTED

SURVIVAL IN FREEZING CONDITIONS

Feeling cold doesn't sound dangerous but, in extreme conditions, it can be fatal. Cold air, wind and water all chill the body. When you start to shiver, it is a sign that your body is losing heat faster than it can replace it. If your core body temperature drops below its normal temperature of 36.8° centigrade, hypothermia sets in.

The stages of hypothermia

MILD – body temperature 35-32°C

At the first stage of hypothermia you will start to shiver, and your body's thermostat orders heat to be drawn inwards from your fingers and toes. Your hands and feet will stiffen and start to turn blue. As your core body temperature drops, heat is also drawn from your head. This will slow down your brain, and your speech will become slurred. You may become confused and angry.

MODERATE – body temperature 32-28°C

At this stage, you will have stopped shivering and worrying about your situation. Your muscles will become rigid and your heartbeat will be uneven. Your only hope now is to add heat from another source as your body has lost its ability to reheat.

SEVERE – body temperature below 28°C

This is the final stage of hypothermia. You will be deeply unconscious, breathing slowly and your heart will be slowing down.

Understanding hypothermia

The body loses heat in four different ways. It's important to understand them so that you can prevent hypothermia.

Evaporation	We lose heat when we breathe or sweat.
Radiation	If your body is warmer than the outside temperature, you will start to cool down.
Conduction	If you are touching something, your body heat will flow into it. Extremely cold air and water can take heat away from the body.
Convection	Wind will take heat away from the body.

How does a pencil sharpener work?

1

2

3

First lessons in surfing

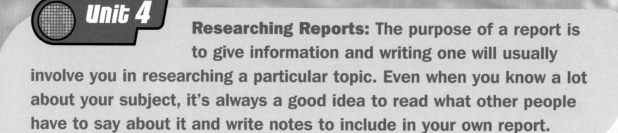

Castle Museum
The Eye of York, off Tower Street

During the eighteenth century, two prisons were built on the site of York Castle: the Debtors Prison and the Female Prison. These two buildings now contain one of York's most interesting museums.

The Castle Museum was founded by Dr John Kirk. As he visited his patients during the late nineteenth century, he realised that the way they lived was changing, so he started to collect everyday items before they disappeared completely. The street and room settings bring these objects to life and show how they would have been used.

The Military Gallery features battles fought in Yorkshire between the eighth and seventeenth centuries. An eighth-century Anglo-Saxon helmet found during excavations in Coppergate, which is very close to the Museum, is displayed here, along with armour and weapons. In the Special Exhibition Gallery, you can see how the Second World War affected the people of York. Gas masks, ration books and clothes are all on display.

In the Children's Gallery, there are teddy bears, board games, jigsaws and dolls that your parents and grandparents might have played with. Sindy, Barbie and Action Man bring the exhibition up to date.

Kirkgate, a Victorian Street

Walk through two Victorian streets, rebuilt using real shop fronts and buildings, rescued from all over the country. Call into Terry's sweet shop, look in the window of William Alexander's bookshop at the first children's books most people could afford to buy, and admire the huge Hansom Cab in Kirkgate. These cabs were used as taxis in Victorian times and are named after their inventor, Joseph Hansom of York.

From *The City of York: A Guidebook* by Gill Matthews

Bibliography and Further Reading

Children's Games by Imogen Opel (Harcourt, 1980)
Coppergate Finds, pamphlet by the York History Society (1974)
Eboracum – Roman York by J Greenwood (York Press, 1993)
Our Debt to Dr Kirk by B. Ansom (Rigby, 1986)
York Through the Ages by Anne Goodyer (Simmons, 1999)

CORAL REEFS

CITIES IN THE SEA

Bees build hives. Beavers build dams. Birds build nests. That's all pretty impressive, but who are the greatest animal architects of all? They might just be coral polyps – little creatures that live in the warm, shallow parts of the Earth's oceans.

CORAL POLYPS

There are nearly a thousand coral species, most of which are less than 2.5cm long although some do grow to about 30cm. The structure of the coral polyp's body is very simple, like a tube. One end attaches itself to a hard surface to stop it from floating all over the place. The polyp's mouth and tentacles are at the other end of the 'tube'. By waving its tentacles, the polyp catches tiny plants and animals to eat.

Coral polyps absorb calcium from the ocean water, and nutrients from fish, that help them to grow more quickly. And that's what makes them the architects of the sea bed.

An undersea coral polyp.

CORAL REEFS

CORAL CONSTRUCTION

Calcium is an important mineral, which our bodies use to make bones. Coral polyps use calcium to build their skeletons too. They just do it a little differently.

Coral structures can be quite complex and may remind us of cabbages and trees.

They turn the calcium into a hard substance called limestone, which they deposit outside their bodies. Eventually, the limestone turns into a 'wall' surrounding the polyp. This 'wall' is the polyp's skeleton.

When coral polyps die, their hard skeletons remain and young polyps anchor themselves on the old limestone. In forming their own skeletons, these young polyps build the next layer of limestone.

With layer on layer of limestone, for millions of years, polyps have been busy creating amazing coral reefs under the sea.

SUPERSIZE CITIES

Like the settings for sci-fi films, coral formations come in all sorts of wild, weird and wonderful shapes. Some look like trees; others resemble cabbages or giant brains.

But it's not just their shapes that fascinate people – their size is impressive too. In fact, experts argue that coral reefs are the largest structures built by any species, including humans.

Stretching for 2,000km along the northeast coast of Australia, the Great Barrier Reef is the largest coral reef of all.

SEB'S SHARK NOTES
SHARK BASICS

1. A shark is a type of fish. But unlike ordinary fish, shark skeletons are made of a rubbery substance called cartilage. Prod your nose or ear – they're cartilage too. Cartilage gives a shark a bendy lightweight body.

2. Sharks breathe oxygen dissolved in the water that wafts over their gills. Certain sharks, like the great white, have to swim all the time to keep the water moving. When they stop, they can't breathe, and if they stop for too long they die.

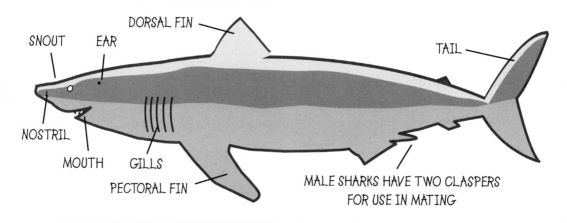

SNOUT   EAR   DORSAL FIN   TAIL   NOSTRIL   MOUTH   GILLS   PECTORAL FIN   MALE SHARKS HAVE TWO CLASPERS FOR USE IN MATING

3. Sharks can be very big, or fairly small. Many sharks are shorter than a man's arm and most them grow less than three metres long.

4. Sharks have large oily livers. Since oil is lighter than water, the liver helps to stop the shark from sinking.

5. Shark skin feels rough because it's made of teeth! The close-packed tiny gnashers are known as denticles.

6. Of the 400 or so different types of shark, the largest, fiercest, and hungriest shark that attacks people is the great white.

From *Wild Lives: Swimming with Sharks* by Nick Arnold

FOSSILS

Fossils are the remains of long-dead animals and plants, turned to stone. They show us that life on Earth was not always the way we see it now. We can learn a certain amount from them, based on what we know of our present world. Fossils found so far only record a tiny part of all the life that has existed on Earth through the ages. All over the world, from China to Patagonia, millions more fossils are waiting to be discovered.

In England, the south coast around Lyme Regis has been declared a World Heritage Site because it is so rich in fossils. Storms and high seas along the coast uncover millions of fossils every winter, and unless they are collected the sea will destroy them. A fossil-collecting code of conduct has been established along the West Dorset coast and a record of Key Scientifically Important Specimens is maintained there.

Fossil sharks' teeth look just like modern ones.

Everyone recognizes ammonites. They are about 200 million years old.

AT HOME WITH THE ALIENS

Be an alien detective! What information can you glean from this alien family's funky living pod? Can you write a report?

The Art of Persuasion: Persuasion is all around us, all the time! For example, TV adverts, food packaging, posters and magazines are all trying to make us buy something, do something or think in a certain way. In this unit you will find out how people go about the 'art of persuasion'.

1. SPORTS SPECIAL

Is your ideal holiday spent learning to play Earth Football, alternating with long days soaking in the sump? Then Club La Tharga is for you!

With its golden climate and multiple facilities, it's perfect for sporting Thargons. Situated on Tharg's northern coast, washed by the purple waters of the Mer Galactica, Club La Tharga will give you a matchless opportunity to recharge your batteries and lubricate your joints. Choose whether to take part in Earth sports, Ancient Thargan games, or Inter-planetary competitions. Then reward yourself for all that action with long soaks in our oil-rejuvenating pools.

2. NATURE LOVERS

A unique opportunity to discover the amazing wildlife and beautiful scenery of Tharg's northern coastline!

The very popular Forest Hotel nestles between the spectacular mountains and shimmering purple sea, in the picturesque village of Tharga. The surrounding countryside teems with wildlife and rare plants – a must for every nature-loving Thargon. The perfect base to explore the Thargos Mountains.

Twin de-charge rooms have private balconies (perfect for early evening twitchers). Facilities include metal fatigue repair rooms (for post-mountaineering relaxation) and daily guided walks.

3. TRIPS FOR TRIBES

Feeling lonely on your own? Can't enjoy yourself unless you are surrounded by all your friends and relations? Can never find a hotel big enough? Worry no more! Club La Tharga's expandable lakeside village of low impact dwellings can be extended in a trice to cater for the whole tribe. Geodesic domes of every size are both comfortable and convenient. The central meeting dome is ideal for hum-alongs and sparking competitions, and the other little pods, all set up for painless de-charging, come in units of two, three and four. Try it and we're sure you'll agree, IT'S HOME FROM HOME IN A DOME.

4. VIRTUAL HOLIDAY

As time passes and our joints start to stiffen, the 'holiday' idea becomes less attractive. Not everyone wants to take part in organized activities. Senior Thargons may like to consider a virtual break instead. Come spend a week in the luxurious divans of Club La Tharga. Hire a headset from Hankis and settle down for zyglots of fascinating travel. Immerse yourself in the historic thrills and spills of the week's games on Planet Football. Venture through the Crystal Caves of the Glass Planet, discovered only recently despite being on Tharg's doorstep. Live life again as a lizard. The choice is yours!

Highland Castle@Wizard Prices

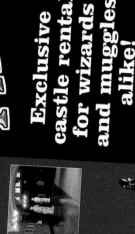

Exclusive castle rental for wizards and muggles alike!

Carbisdale Castle Youth Hostel is a grand castle set in fine woodlands, with a statue gallery, art collection and Ghost.

It's a unique venue for groups of friends, family reunions and special events.

Carbisdale is just one of over 150 Hostels throughout Britain and Ireland available for exclusive hire.

For more information visit RentAHostel.com or call 0870 1 55 32 55 for a free brochure

YOU DON'T HAVE TO BE MADONNA TO ENJOY A HIGHLAND CASTLE WEDDING.

You can rent exclusive use of our Highland castle for a fraction of the normal cost.

Carbisdale Castle Youth Hostel is a fantastic wedding venue. It's a grand castle set in fine woodlands, complete with its own art collection and statue gallery.

Its great value too, exclusive use of the building means you can accommodate all of your guests under one roof at no extra cost. You can arrange for your own caterers and plan the special day you want; we provide the stunning backdrop.

To arrange a viewing or for further information and prices please contact the Manager Jamie Burgess on 0871 330 8509 or visit www.carbisdale.org

DES. RES. NOW AVAILABLE

Set within the desirable New Generation area of Trek Town, this spacious and well presented two de-charge room pod has been finished to a high standard to offer a contemporary living space, including a stunning existence room flooded with planetary light. It boasts state-of-the-art fittings throughout, including a retro-human style 'kitchen'. The pod has its own starship landing point and an internal glass garden.

Situated within moments of the town's main re-fuelling centre, this property would make an ideal purchase for those looking to move up in the planet.

Leasehold. Price on application.

Dear Sir,

I am writing to apply for the position of Estate Agent, as advertised in last week's Tharg Weekly. My career to date has so far included some deep space travel, as I was the youngest member of the team researching Planet Football. I had several close encounters with the natives, and wrote a prize-winning account of the mission.

I feel that I am well qualified for Estate Agency work. I understand the importance of working as a team, and have experience of a wide variety of lifestyles – when on Planet Football I had the chance to inspect a range of alien living arrangements, which certainly made me appreciate the comforts of my home planet. As I have lived in the Sniktrek area for many zyglots, I have a thorough knowledge of all the main attractions, and know the district like the back of my neck.

I hope you will consider this application favourably.

Yours faithfully,

Ariel Galapagob

WATER IS COOL IN SCHOOL

More and more schools are now changing the way they provide drinking water for their pupils. Once, children could only get a drink of water at break time or lunchtime, or by asking permission to go to the cloakroom during lessons. Now, there are water coolers and bottles in classrooms around the country.

Research has shown that we need to drink at least eight glasses of water a day, even more in hot weather. If we don't, we start to dehydrate, our brains cannot work as efficiently and we can get headaches. Scientific studies prove that children who are dehydrated do not concentrate as well as those who drink the recommended amount of water. "If children do not drink enough water they are storing up problems for adulthood, such as kidney disease and high blood pressure," a leading kidney specialist has stated.

Schools too have seen the benefits of supplying their pupils with water. Teachers of a class of 9–10 year-olds in a Merseyside primary school, reported that after only a month of drinking water whenever they wanted to, the children's attention spans improved. One headteacher said that simply stopping for a drink seemed to help children to re-focus on what they were doing. A class teacher said, "The children seem less tired and they seem to enjoy drinking water. I think they find it more refreshing than fizzy pop now." It has also been pointed out that in many schools, the quality of tap water has not improved since the schools were built – over 100 years ago.

Local businesses are also getting involved in providing water to schools. In Yorkshire, a water cooler company has struck a deal with businesses – if they rent three coolers from the company, a local school receives a cooler free. In some areas of Liverpool local supermarkets are providing schools with refillable bottles with sports style spouts, at a discount price.

"We all know that we should drink more water," said a spokeswoman for the National Kidney Research Fund. "The idea of allowing children to drink water in classrooms starts a good habit for life."

PROVAMEL FROM

alpro soya

DAIRY FREE
NON-GMO SOYA BEANS

Soya Dream

Sainsbury's

low price

long life
orange juice
made with concentrated
orange juice

Sainsbury's
Taste the Diffe

Sainsbury's West Country FREE RANGE CHICKEN

2 Fresh West Country Free Range Chicken Breast Fillets

Grade A

This free range chicken has access to tree-planted fields, is raised on small West Country farms and fed on a wheat-based diet which includes whole grain to enhance flavour and texture.

Keep Refrigerated		Ideal for home freezing
Display until		Use by
15 DEC		15 DEC
Weight		Pack price
0.296 kg		£ 3.99
Price per kg		Packaged in a protective atmosphere.
£ 13.49		Once opened consume within 24 hours.

0217110003993 21:29 05 4

See reverse for nutritional information, food safety tips, cooking instructions.
Sainsbury's Careline Freephone 0800 636262. Produced in the UK for Sainsbury's Supermarkets Ltd, 33 Holborn, London EC1N 2HT. Internet www.sainsburys.co.uk

M0023

Nestle® LIVE LIKE A **Rol** Pop Idol
Discover the power of the Last Rolo
VIP WEEKEND BREAKS. 10 TO BE WON

Sainsbury's
blue Parrot café

fruit in jelly
chopped juicy peaches
in an orange flavour jelly

Sainsbury's
TUNA STEAK
DOLPHIN FRIENDLY

in sunflower oil

THE LORD OF THE RINGS
THE RETURN OF THE KING

INSTANT WIN
Plus FREE 3-D Cards offer

330ml e

Perfect PORK

Tender and **Succulent**
2 Pork Loin Steaks

12 mins	280c	DEC 7	£1.71
	6,11	DEC 7	

NEW

Hello, it's Prof here again bringing you one of my greatest inventions. The other day I was watching my assistant trying to cram a large box of Weetos into his lunch box when it struck me...
...My next invention should be the **WEETOS BAR!**

CRUNCHY BUBBLY WEETOS AND OODLES OF REAL **MILK CHOCOLATE**

Weetos

THE MOST **CHOCORIFFIC** BAR A'ROUND!

MADE WITH REAL FRUIT
NATURAL COLOURS
3 X ITS OWN WEIGHT IN FRUIT
GOOD FOR ENERGY
NO ARTIFICIAL FLAVOURS
LOW IN FAT

IDEAL FOR LUNCHBOXES

FRUIT BOWL

school bars

Lunchbox

Each school bar® is made from more than three times its own weight in real fruit, which is then dried and concentrated into puree.

school bars® are perfect for lunch boxes and as part of a healthy nutritious diet.

school bars® are gluten free, lactose free and suitable for vegetarians.

INGREDIENTS:
Fruit (47%) (consisting of concentrated apple puree (17%), pear puree, and dehydrated apple (22%)), Sugar, Maltodextrin, Glucose syrup, Vegetable oil, Natural colour (chlorophyllin), Gelling agent (pectin), Malic acid, Milk protein, Flavouring.

NUTRITIONAL INFORMATION	PER 100g	PER 20g serving
ENERGY		
PROTEIN		
CARBOHYDRATE		
OF WHICH SUGARS		
FAT		
OF WHICH SATURATES		
FIBRE		
SODIUM		

5 060011 810079

Fruit Bowl® and school bars® are registered trademarks of Stream Foods
Stream Foods Ltd, Unit 5, Broadend Industrial Estate,
Walsoken, WISBECH, Cambs PE14 7BQ

Sainsbury's **Blueberries**

fresh

This sweet, aromatic berry is ideal for snacking, garnishing and cooking

Packed for Sainsbury's Supermarkets Ltd, 33 Holborn, London EC1N 2HT Freephone 0800 636262 www.sainsburys.co.uk

Keep refrigerated after purchase Serve at room temperature for the very best flavour	Wash thoroughly before use	A0800 L15
Display Until		
03 AUG	Weight	
Origin	150g e	0101 5423
POL	BLUE CROP	

buy any 2 for £2
blueberries 150g,
redcurrants 150g,
blackberries 150g

WaterAid/Jon Spaull

World Water Day:
22 March

BUCKETS OF
pennies FOR
BUCKETS OF
water

22 March is World Water Day; the UN designated day to consider world water issues such as global access to safe drinking water.

In many parts of Africa and Asia collecting domestic water is a full time job that often falls to children. Hundreds of thousands of children, mainly girls, are denied the chance of an education simply because most of their day is spent walking miles to collect water from a traditional water source – often a filthy pool, full of diseases.

WaterAid, the UK's specialist water development charity, works to help communities in Africa and Asia establish clean water supplies close to home, such as village wells fitted with handpumps. This means that children no longer have to walk miles to collect water and have the time to go to school.

WaterAid's school video *Buckets of Water* explains the issue in more detail by following the lives of two children, Christina and Akolgo, in Ghana. The video is suitable for 7 to 11 year olds and is available on free loan for a month – please order your copy now.

Your school can also help children in Africa and Asia by organising a World Water Day fundraising activity to raise buckets of pennies for WaterAid. It costs just over £10 per head to provide a community with a sustainable source of clean, safe water. Perhaps the pupils could organise a 'river of pennies' in the playground, a **welly throwing competition**, a **sponsored swim** or a simple **bucket collection** at school. We can provide further watery fundraising ideas. After the event please send a cheque made out to 'WaterAid (Buckets of Water Appeal)' and we will send you a certificate of achievement to be displayed at school.

www.wateraid.org.uk

WaterAid

WaterAid – Water for life
THE UK'S ONLY MAJOR CHARITY DEDICATED EXCLUSIVELY TO THE PROVISION OF SAFE DOMESTIC WATER, SANITATION AND HYGIENE PROMOTION TO THE WORLD'S POOREST PEOPLE

Response form:

Please fax back now on **020 7793 4545**
Or send to: **WaterAid, Buckets of Water Appeal, Prince Consort House, 27-29 Albert Embankment, London, SE1 7UB**

Please accept our donation of £
Cheques made payable to **WaterAid (Buckets of Water Appeal)**

School

Contact Name

Address

Postcode

Please send me the materials ticked below:
☐ World Water Day Fundraising Pack
☐ Buckets of Water Video – for 7–11 year olds (on one month loan)
☐ Information on WaterAid speaker for your School Assembly

Alternatively call on **020 7793 4563** or email: **schools@WaterAid.org.uk**

☐ WaterAid and WaterAid Trading Ltd may like to send you further information. If you do NOT wish to receive this, please tick this box.

Charity registration no. 288701

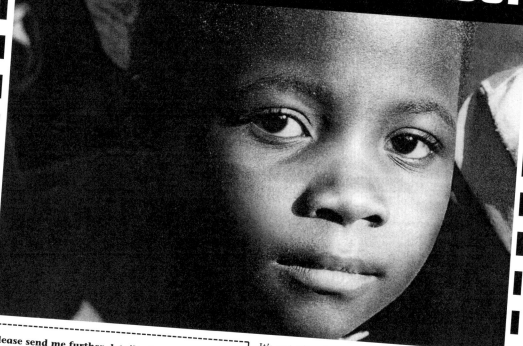

Sponsorship can change your life too.

Please send me further details about sponsoring a child, or call 01460 23 80 80.

I'm interested in sponsoring in:

❑ Africa ❑ Asia ❑ Where need is greatest

Mr/Mrs/Miss/Ms

Address

_____

Postcode _____

Tel(Day) _____

(Eve) _____

I can't sponsor a child now, but enclose a gift of: 200109

❑ £200 ❑ £100 ❑ £50 ❑ £25 ❑ £

ActionAid and our subsidiaries may contact you with more information about our activities. If you do not wish to receive this information, please tick this box ❑

Make cheques / POs payable to ActionAid, and send to:
ActionAid,
FREEPOST BS4868,
Chard,
Somerset TA20 1BR

www.actionaid.org

act:onaid

It's not often in life you feel as if you can really make a difference. Especially when it comes to the problems facing the developing world.

With ActionAid, if you sponsored a child like Ambia you would be helping a whole community. Sponsorship that helps provide access to safe, clean water, healthcare and education.

ActionAid believe that only when these rights, which we take for granted, have been secured can children and their families begin to focus on developing a self-sufficient future.

You'll actually be aware of the difference you're making to a child's community with regular updates from local fieldworkers and messages from the child you sponsor.

Contact ActionAid today and in return we'll send you an information pack with a photo of a child awaiting your sponsorship.

Fill in the coupon and bring change to everyone's life.

Delving into Dictionaries: Dictionaries don't have to be dull! Of course, the usual ones help you to find out what words mean. But others define technical expressions in subjects you might be interested in, like computing, or tell you what everyday sayings mean.

A DICTIONARY OF PORTMANTEAU WORDS

Portmanteau words blend two words or sounds together to form a new word. 'Chortle' (from *chuckle* and *snort*) was the first portmanteau word and was used by Lewis Carroll in his book *Through the Looking Glass*. The word 'portmanteau' means a travelling bag that divides into two parts.

animatronics (noun) technique of making and moving lifelike robots for use in films (*animated + electronics*)

breathalyser (noun) device used to measure the amount of alcohol in the breath (*breath + analyse*)

brunch (noun) a late morning meal (*breakfast + lunch*)

camcorder (noun) a portable machine that records moving pictures (*camera + recorder*)

chocoholic (noun) a person who is addicted to chocolate (*chocolate + alcoholic*)

chortle (verb) to laugh in a gleeful way (*chuckle + snort*)

docusoap (noun) a film that follows a real life situation over a period of time (*documentary + soap opera*)

electrocute (verb) to injure or kill someone by an electric shock (*electricity + execute*)

ginormous (adjective) extremely large (*gigantic + enormous*)

guesstimate (noun) an estimate based on a mixture of a guess and calculation (*guess + estimate*)

hoolivan
(noun) a police van carrying camera equipment for observing crowd behaviour at football matches
(hooligan + van)

identitikit (noun) a picture of a person reconstructed from typical facial features following the description of a witness
(identity + kit)

motel (noun) roadside hotel for motorists *(motor + hotel)*

motorcade (noun) a procession of cars *(motor + cavalcade)*

pixel (noun) a tiny area on a screen
(picture + element)

prequel (noun) a story or film that contains events that happened before an existing work
(pre + sequel)

pulsar (noun) a spinning star that sends out regular pulses of radio waves
(pulsating + star)

smog (noun) a thick polluted mist
(smoke + fog)

telethon (noun) a very long television programme, usually designed to raise money for charity
(television + marathon)

transistor (noun) a small electrical part, usually in a radio or television
(transfer + resistor)

twigloo (noun) a tree house, usually used by environmental protestors
(twig + igloo)

I SAY, I SAY, I SAY

Sayings or proverbs and idioms are often used in everyday speech. These words and phrases often don't mean exactly what they say but the ideas in them are understandable.

Cat

❓ Curiosity killed the cat.

✅ *Being curious can get you into trouble.*

❓ While the cat's away, the mice will play.

✅ *When the person in charge is not there, people will do as they please.*

❓ The cat's whiskers

✅ *The very best*

❓ Not enough room to swing a cat

✅ *A very small space*

Crab

❓ You cannot make a crab walk straight.

✅ *Don't attempt to do the impossible.*

Dog

❓ Love me, love my dog.

✅ *Anyone who wants to be my friend has to accept me faults and all.*

❓ Why keep a dog and bark yourself?

✅ *There is no point in doing a job yourself if you have someone to do it for you.*

❓ A dog's dinner

✅ *A terrible mess*

Hair

❓ To tear your hair out

✅ *To be really frustrated*

❓ To get in someone's hair

✅ *To really annoy someone*

Head

❓ Two heads are better than one.

✅ *In times of trouble, it is better to ask for help rather than carry on alone.*

❓ To laugh your head off

✅ *To laugh uncontrollably*

Leap
Q Look before you leap.
Q *Think carefully about something before you do it.*

Leg
Q To pull someone's leg
Q *To tease a person by telling them something untrue*

Q To talk the hind leg off a donkey
Q *To talk non-stop*

Mouse
Q Don't make yourself a mouse or the cat will eat you.
Q *Don't be so timid that people take advantage of you.*

Pen
Q The pen is mightier than the sword.
Q *Writing can be more powerful than fighting.*

Penny
Q In for a penny, in for a pound
Q *If you are going to do something, do it well.*

Q Look after the pennies and the pounds will look after themselves.

Q *If you take care of small things, that will take care of bigger things.*

Q The penny drops
Q *To understand something at last*

Q To turn up like a bad penny
Q *Said about someone who is not liked who keeps turning up*

Sneezed
Q Not to be sneezed at
Q *An offer that is too good to refuse*

Storm
Q A storm in a tea cup
Q *A lot of fuss about nothing*

Swings
Q What you lose on the swings, you gain on the roundabouts.
Q *Things usually balance out in the end.*

Tongue
Q To hold your tongue
Q *To keep quiet*

Weather
Q Under the weather
Q *Feeling unwell*

Work
Q All work and no play makes Jack a dull boy.
Q *You won't do your work well if you don't have some fun.*

A-Z OF COMPUTING

» **attachment** (noun) any file that is sent with an email message

» **bit** (from binary digit) the smallest unit of data stored in a computer (as a single binary digit of 0 or 1)

» **bug** (noun) an error in a computer program

» **byte** (noun) a unit of information stored in a computer, equal to eight bits

» **command** (noun) an order given to the computer's operating system or to control software

» **cursor** (noun) the mouse pointer, hand or flashing line that shows where you are on the computer screen

» **database** (noun) a collection of similar information stored in a file, for example, a database of addresses

» **device** (noun) equipment attached to the computer through the control box

» **digital camera** (noun) a camera that records digital images, and sometimes video clips, in its memory so that they can then be downloaded onto a computer

» **email** (noun) electronic mail, the sending and receiving of information from one computer to another connected by the Internet

» **file** (noun) a collection of data or a program stored in a computer

» **input** (noun) a signal sent in to the computer or the device that sends it

» **Internet** (noun) an information network that is accessed by telephone lines and connects computers around the world

» HOW TO SAY THE WORD   » HOW TO USE THE WORD

» **instruction** (noun) an order that a computer can understand and carry out

» **kilobyte** (noun) a unit of computer memory or data equal to approximately one thousand bytes

» **output** (noun) a signal sent from the computer or the device to which it is sent

» **procedure** (noun) a set of instructions that makes a computer do a task

» **RAM** (acronym for random access memory) the computer memory that holds data and programs while they are running

» **ROM** (acronym for read only memory) the computer memory that holds programs or data permanently

» **sequence** (noun) an ordered set of instructions

» **spacebar** (noun) the longest key on the keyboard. It makes a space between characters.

» **surf** (verb) move from site to site on the Internet

» **toggle** (verb) to switch between two computer settings

» **URL** (abbreviation for Uniform Resource Locator) the standard way of giving the location of a web page on the Internet

» **virus** (noun) a piece of computer code introduced secretly into a computer to destroy data

» **website** (noun) a set of pages on the Internet that belong to one person or group

» **World Wide Web** (noun) a system that links Internet sites together so you can surf for information by clicking from one site to another

» **zip** (verb) to condense a program or data so that it occupies less memory

INDEX

48

Literacy World

Essential Non-fiction

An anthology of exciting non-fiction compiled by
Sylvia Karavis and **Gill Matthews**

How does an alien cheat at football? Why are coral reefs called
'Cities in the Sea'? And why might someone say, "Love me, love
my dog"? Want to find out? Then read on – here's a wild and
wonderful anthology of non-fiction to trigger your imagination!

This *Essential Non-fiction* anthology has been carefully put together
to give you some of the very best examples of different non-fiction
writing. We hope you enjoy it.

Non-fiction anthology

Series consultant:
Rachael Sutherland

STAGE 3

ISBN 0-435-15770-1

9 780435 157708